Spa
Pe

Also available from Macmillan Children's Books

Crazy Mayonnaisy Mum
Poems by Julia Donaldson
Illustrated by Nick Sharratt

There's a Hamster in the Fast Lane
Poems chosen by Brian Moses

Pirate Poems
By David Harmer

Read Me 1 and 2
A Poem For Every Day Of The Year
Chosen by Gaby Morgan

Read Me and Laugh
A Funny Poem For Every Day Of The Year
Chosen by Gaby Morgan

Space Poems

Chosen by
Gaby Morgan

Illustrated by
Jane Eccles

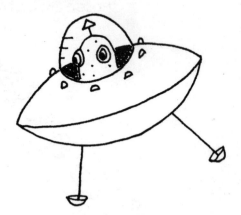

Macmillan Children's Books

For Jude Weston
– future space explorer –
and Lauren, Fliss and Talya,
the heroines of publishing
Space Command!

First published 2006 by Macmillan Children's Books
a division of Macmillan Publishers Limited
20 New Wharf Road, London N1 9RR
Basingstoke and Oxford
Associated companies throughout the world
www.panmacmillan.com

ISBN 978-0-330-44057-8

7 9 8

A CIP catalogue record for this book is available from the British Library.

Printed and bound by CPI Group (UK) Ltd, Croydon, CR0 4YY

Contents

Space Counting Rhyme

10 flying saucers, 10 flashing lights
 9 glowing trails, 9 meteorites
 8 silver spaceships trying to find
 7 lost aliens left behind
 6 burning comets blazing fire
 5 red rockets blasting higher
 4 satellites, 4 radar dishes
 3 stars shooting means 3 wishes
 2 bright lights – the moon and sun
 1 little me to shine upon

Paul Cookson

The Star

Twinkle, twinkle, little star,
How I wonder what you are!
Up above the world so high,
Like a diamond in the sky.

When the blazing sun is gone,
When he nothing shines upon,
Then you show your little light,
Twinkle, Twinkle, all the night.

Then the traveller in the dark,
Thanks you for your tiny spark,
He could not see which way to go,
If you did not twinkle so.

In the dark blue sky you keep,
And often through my curtains peep,
For you never shut your eye,
Till the sun is in the sky.

As your bright and tiny spark,
Lights the traveller in the dark –
Though I know not what you are,
Twinkle, twinkle, little star.

Jane Taylor

Star Travelling

I'm a twinkling eye
I'm a dancing light,
I'm a tiny snowdrop
I'm a splash of white.

I'm a dash of silver
I'm a jewel too far,
I'm a wish still waiting
I'm a shooting star.

Andrew Collett

Star Wish

Starlight. Starbright.
First star I see tonight.
I wish I may, I wish I might
Have the wish I wish tonight.

Traditional

The Planets

In the middle
is the Sun,

Then comes Mercury,
number one.

Venus next is number two,
and then a planet spinning blue:

The Earth, our home,
is number three.

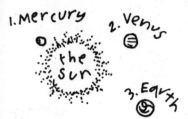

1. Mercury

the sun

2. Venus

3. Earth

8. Neptune

Look through the stars,
what do we see?

6. Saturn

Red desert Mars
is number four

Of all the planets,
then there's more.

Jupiter is number five,
after that we will arrive

9

At Saturn's rings
for number six.

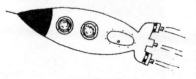

Moving on
we quickly slip

To Uranus at number seven,
out there in the misty heaven.

Then Neptune waits
at number eight:

So all the planets make a line
and Pluto's last at number nine!

Dave Ward

It is hard to count the stars

One

Two

Three

Four

Have I counted you before?

Four

Five

Six

Ten

Perhaps I should begin again

Philip Burton

The View from Space

How beautiful Earth looks from here:
It hangs a precious, perfect sphere.
Set against vast and silent space
It seems a welcoming, warm place.

Ahead, an endless unknown story:
Star-sprinkled blackness, a cold glory.
Behind, and fading, Earth's sweet
    song:
There, where life is, I belong.

Eric Finney

Seeing Stars

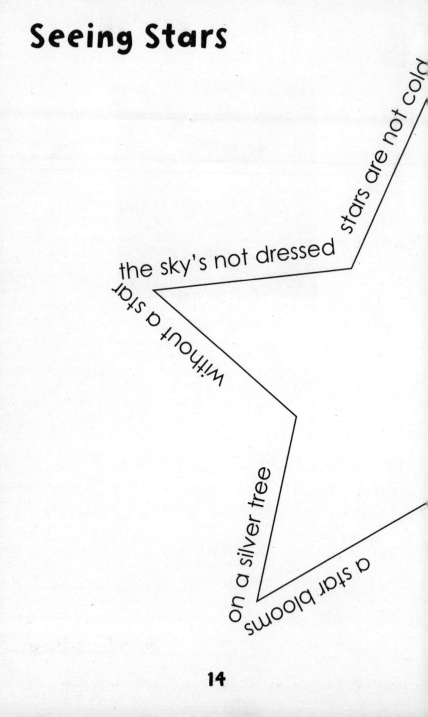

stars are not cold
the sky's not dressed
without a star
on a silver tree
a star blooms

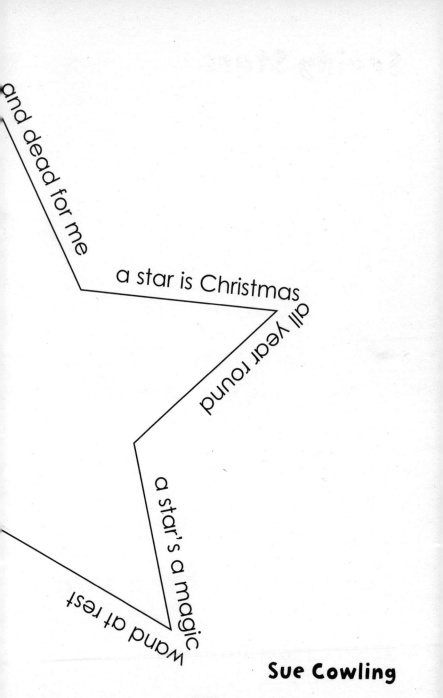

and dead for me

a star is Christmas

all year round

a star's a magic

wand at rest

Sue Cowling

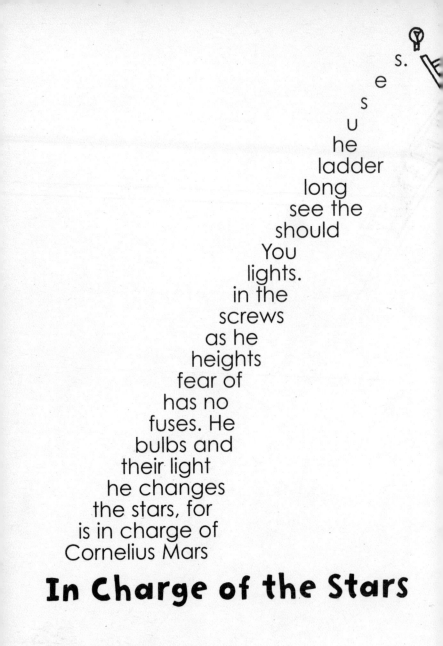

s.
e
s
u
he
ladder
long
see the
should
You
lights.
in the
screws
as he
heights
fear of
has no
fuses. He
bulbs and
their light
he changes
the stars, for
is in charge of
Cornelius Mars

In Charge of the Stars

Robert Scotellaro

The Space Cross Code

(Practising it will staggeringly increase your chances of returning safely from a space-walk)

Look round and round and round and round and round and round,
Look round and round and round and round,
Look round and round and round and round round,
For you won't hear a sound.

Look round and round and round again
Then dash across the void
And watch out for that speeding probe,
Comet or asteroid!

Philip Waddell

Brief Encounter

Zooming on and on
Through space,
I want to see
A Martian's face,
And when I've said,
"Hallo," well then
I want to zoom
Back home again.

Clive Webster

On a Sphere of Blue

On a sphere of blue
marbled with white
taking a trip
through silent night,

out for a spin
in starry space
go me and you
and the human race.

Robert Hull

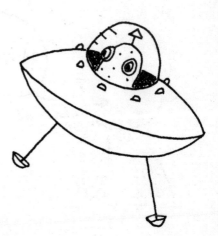

Our Spaceship

Make me a spaceship Dad,
one that will really fly.
Make me a spaceship Dad,
let's take off into the sky.

Let's take a trip to the moon,
let's play games on Mars,
let's take off once again
and visit all the stars.

Make me a spaceship Dad,
one that will really fly.
We'll have such fun in space
just you and I.

Brian Moses

Footprints on the Moon

There were men on the moon once.
They travelled through space
and found that the moon
was a dry, dusty place.

They collected some moon rocks
and had a look round
and left lots of footprints
there on the ground.

They couldn't stay long
as the moon has no air,
but the footprints they left
in the dust are still there.

Marian Swinger

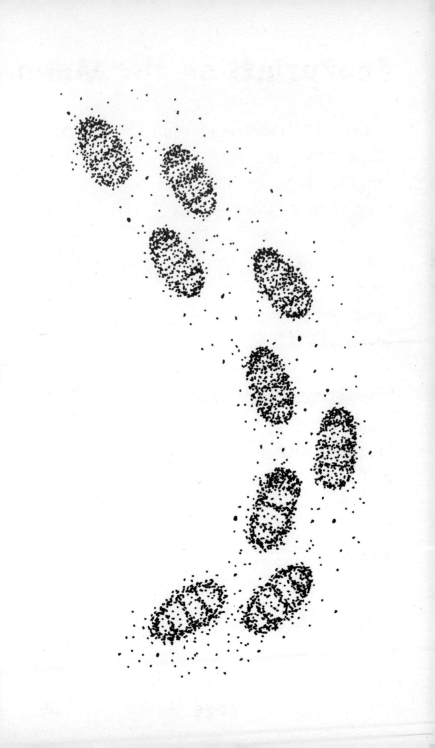

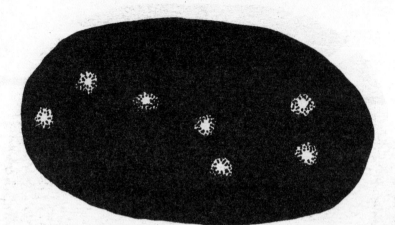

Space

Stuffed with stars
Packed with planets
Abundant in asteroids
Crammed with constellations
Endlessly expanding?

Philip Waddell

The Visitor

From beyond
the Solar System,
from deep
in Outer Space,
a visitor with
a long, bright tail
came to show
its fiery face!

Racing towards
our planet,
faster than
a rocket ship
the comet zoomed,
then turned around
to start its
return trip.

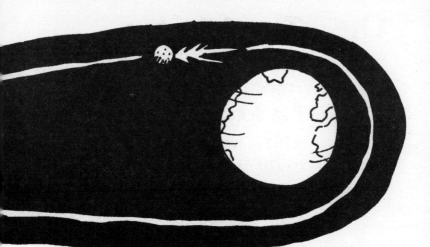

Following
its orbit,
going back
from where it came,
but a hundred years
or so from now
it'll visit
us again!

Tony Langham

The Alien

On my way to school I saw an alien.
No you didn't, said Billy

I saw an alien with two heads.
No you didn't, said Jake

I saw an alien with two heads and
    four arms.
No you didn't, said Ed

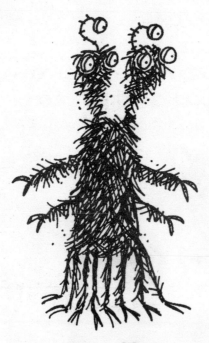

I saw an alien with two heads, four
    arms and six eyes.
No you didn't, said Harriet

I saw an alien with two heads, four
    arms, six eyes and eight legs.
No you didn't, said Ali

OH YES HE DID,
Said the alien

And everyone said

aaaaaaaaaAAAAAAAA
HHHHHHHH

Roger Stevens

Gravity

If it wasn't for earth's
gravitational pull
then objects would float up
and skies would be full
of ripe conkers, bombs, cow-dung,
those pencils we lose
from coat pockets, high jumpers
like large kangaroos,
confetti, leaves, litter,
a melee of fruit,
all those sticks thrown for puppies
and the footballs we boot.
Imagine: this planet
a much tidier place.

But think of that mess up in space.

Rachel Rooney

My Spaceship

I've a picture of Pluto,
    My white spacesuit,
        My robot Charlie,
            My red moon boots,
                All hidden tight
                    In my secret lair,
My spaceship under the stairs.

Not even Mum,
    Nor my sister Sal,
        Not even Dad,
            Nor my brother Cal,
                Can come with me
                    To my secret lair,
My spaceship under the stairs.

I can jet to the moon,
  Or fly to Mars,
    Take my shuttle,
      Or my solar car,
        Shout, "We have lift-off!"
         On a faraway star,
In my spaceship under the stairs.

I can catch a comet,
  Or a meteorite,
    Zoom round and round,
      A satellite,
        Do what I want,
          Whenever I like,
In my spaceship under the stairs.

It's my special place,
  When I creep inside,
    To play or think,
      To dream or hide,
        Or just to be there,
          With my old cloth bear,
In my spaceship under the stairs.

Mary Green

Space Station Lullaby

Hush, little astronaut in your berth.
Don't wish you were back in bed on
   Earth!
You'll sleep as soundly here in space –
A strap will hold you firmly in place.
With these dark shades upon your
   eyes
You won't see the sunset-rise-set-rise
And wear your earmuffs so the rest of
   the crew
Can do their work without disturbing
   you.

Sue Cowling

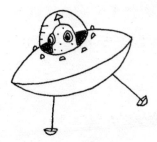

The Owl and the Astronaut

The owl and the astronaut
Sailed through space
In their intergalactic ship.
They kept hunger at bay
With three pills a day
And drank through a protein drip.
The owl dreamed of mince
And slices of quince
And remarked how life had gone flat;
"It may be all right
To fly faster than light
But I preferred the boat and the cat."

Gareth Owen

The Alien's Sweet Shop

He sells Asteroid Crunch
And Galaxy Munch
And Flying Saucer Dips.

He has Chocolate Zooms
And Peppermint Moons
And Spaceship Lollies to lick.

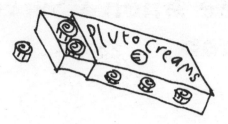

There are Pluto Creams
And Jupiter Dreams
And Twinkling Stardust Bars.

But his Milky Way Treats
That are heaven to eat
Are my favourite sweets by far.

Cynthia Rider

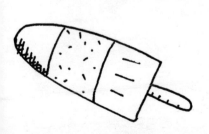

Space

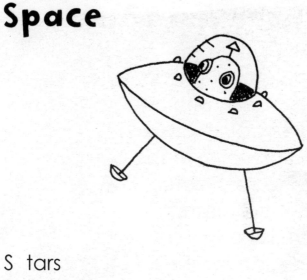

S tars
P lanets
A steroids
C onstellations
E xtraterrestrials

Celia Gentles

Where Am I?

There are mountains here, and craters,
and places with beautiful names:
The Bay of Rainbows,
The Lake of Dreams,
The Sea of Nectar,
The Sea of Tranquillity.
There is no water
in the seas or the lakes.

The hottest days
are hotter than boiling water.
The nights are colder
than anywhere on Earth.

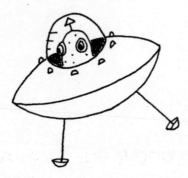

I can see stars very clearly,
and nearer than them,
something wonderful. Imagine
a huge blue and white marble
glowing in a black sky.

Wendy Cope

My Rocket Dreamed...

My rocket dreamed of circling the
   earth,
orbiting the moon,
zigzagging planets,
looping the loop with satellites,
dodging meteorites,
racing comets
and disappearing into time warps
   and black holes.

Instead, it circled the garden shed,
orbited the swing,
zigzagged the apple tree,
looped the loop with the clothes line,
dodged two butterflies,
raced one wasp and a bluebottle
then disappeared over the hedge
into the time warp and black hole
that is Mr Hislop's back garden.

Paul Cookson

First Star

Starlight, starbright,
First star that I see tonight:
From Earth, fantastically far,
I make my wishes on a star.

I wish for a world at peace
Where wars and hatred cease.
I wish for a world that's fair
Whose people give and share.
I wish for a world that's clean:
Cared-for, unspoilt, green.
I wish my life to be,
With friends and family,
Loyal, loving, caring,
Adventurous and daring.

On the first star of the night,
Go wishes, go, take flight.

Eric Finney

In A Spin!

The Moon goes round the Earth,
And the Earth goes round the Sun,
And me, I just go round and round . . .
Wondering how it's done!

Graham Denton

Star Gazing

I've got a telescope to look at the stars
I can see planets like Venus and Mars.
I'll look at the Moon with its smiling face

Or stare out at the blackness

of deepest space!

Chris Ogden

Earthset

Night spreads like purple heather
over wasteland sky
and marbled earth rolls gently into
    sleep.

Judith Nicholls

The Really Rocking Rocket Trip

We're off in a rocket
A silver, shiny rocket
Zooming in our rocket
Just you and me
Racing in our rocket
Our really rocking rocket
Rolling in our rocket
What a lot we'll see!

Land on Jupiter, play with some
   aliens
Land on Neptune, swim in the sea
Land on Venus, play kissy-kissy chase
Land on Mars, chocolate bars in
   every tree
Land on Mercury, take the
   temperature
Land on Saturn, cos it's Saturday
Land on Uranus, play tiggy in our
   spacesuits
Land on Pluto, hip-hip-hooray!

Back to our rocket
Our wonderful rocket
Away in our rocket
Just you and me
Blast off in our rocket
Our supersonic rocket
Land in the garden
Just in time for tea!

David Harmer

Moon

"The moon is thousands of miles
    away,"
My Uncle Trevor said.
Why can't he see
It's caught in a tree
Above our onion bed?

Gareth Owen

The Space Creator's Playground

The other day, way out in space,
Somewhere over France,
All the stars and planets
Held a spaciversary dance.

A trillion billion years ago
The Space Creator sang,
"I'll make a planet playground
And I'll make it with a BANG!"

He made it with a BANG
And he saw that it was good,
Sun and moon and stars and earth
All forming as they should.

So spin, you planets, shoot, you stars,
Jump along Jupiter, Move along
   Mars,
Bungee-bear, bounce and bop,
Dance round space and never stop,

The Space Creator's playground
Is spinning as it should.
He made it with a BANG
And he saw that it was good.

Daphne Kitching

On Some Other Planet

On some other planet
near some other star,
there's a music-loving alien
with a big estate car.

On some other planet,
on some far-distant world,
there's a bright sunny garden
where a cat lies curled.

On some other planet
a trillion miles away,
there are parks and beaches
where the young aliens play.

On some other planet
in another time zone,
there are intelligent beings
who feel very much alone.

On some other planet,
one that we can't see,
there must be one person
who's a duplicate of me.

John Rice

Twinkle, Twinkle

Twinkle, twinkle, far-off star
I think I know just what you are,
a great, colossal ball of fire,
higher than the sky, much higher,
a giant gas burner, ever bright,
like a furnace in the night.

Marian Swinger

Shed in Space

My Grandad Lewis
On my mother's side
Had two ambitions.
One was to take first prize
For shallots at the village show
And the second
Was to be a space commander.
Every Tuesday,
After I'd got their messages,
He'd lead me with a wink
To his garden shed
And there, amongst the linseed
And the sacks of peat and horse
    manure,
He'd light his pipe
And settle in his deckchair.
His old eyes on the blue and distant
That no one else could see,
He'd ask,
"Are we A-OK for lift off?"

Gripping the handles of the lawn
    mower
I'd reply:
"A-OK."
And then
Facing the workbench,
In front of shelves of paint and
    creosote
And racks of glistening chisels,
He'd talk to Mission Control.
"Five-Four-Three-Two-One-Zero –
We have lift off.
This is Grandad Lewis talking,
Do you read me?
Britain's first space shed
Is rising majestically into orbit
From its launch pad
In the allotments
In Lakey Lane."

And so we'd fly,
Through timeless afternoons
Till teatime came,
Amongst the planets
And mysterious suns,
While the world
Receded like a dream:
Grandad never won
That prize for shallots,
But as the captain
Of an intergalactic shed
There was no one to touch him.

Gareth Owen

Rocket Boy

At night
I am captain
of an alien crew,
in my red and silver rocket
speeding

through stars.
Behind closed eyes
I, the bold explorer,
fly past pulsing purple planets,
spinning

with rings,
emerald moons.
I dodge space dust, comets,
bronze and gold starbursts, red giants,
white dwarfs.

At night
I am captain
of an alien crew
till I'm sucked inside the black hole
of sleep.

Celia Gentles

Some Facts About Stars

The hotter the star, the bluer it shines.
The smaller the star, the longer it lives.
It shouldn't be hard to remember
    these lines
(The hotter the star, the bluer it
    shines).
You can search the night sky for
    meaningful signs,
Or study it just for the pleasure it
    gives.
The hotter the star, the bluer it shines,
The smaller the star, the longer it lives.

Wendy Cope

Shooting Stars

Shooting stars
pierce the night,
streaks of gold,
rods of light.
Make a wish
as they fly,
while you watch
starry eyed.

Marian Swinger

Jumping on the Moon

When you jump on Earth
You land with a thud
In the mud

When you jump on the moon
You soar like a balloon
You glide like a feather
on a summer afternoon
You float like a ballet dancer
in a graceful arc
You land like a dandelion clock
in the park

Roger Stevens

Clean Space

Sweep
up that star
dust and tidy your moon,
wash your black
holes

and use
the vacuum –
fast! or your rocket money
will be a thing of
the past.

Liz Brownlee

Spaceship Shop

I need to find a spaceship shop
I want to buy a rocket
One that's sleek and shiny
With a key so I can lock it

My aim is to travel
As high as I can go
Then land on a peaceful planet
Leap out and say "Hello!"

I won't stay in space too long
With bright stars all around me
I know if I'm not home on time
Mum is bound to ground me

But first I need to find that spaceship
   shop
So I can buy a rocket
One that's sleek and shiny
With a key so I can lock it

Note: Make sure that its brakes work
       I'll crash if I can't stop it!

Bernard Young

Lullaby for an Alien

Hush-a-bye, sky baby,
As we float through spangled space.
Mamma knit your shawl from
    moonbeams,
Sewed stardust in the lace.

Don't cry now, sweet sky baby,
See the glittering planets spin.
Daddy wove your crib from
    sunbeams,
You're rocked by solar winds.

Close your eyes, sky baby,
Shush, shush now, can't you hear
The planets humming nursery rhymes
Not meant for human ears?

One day you'll ride on comets,
You'll somersault the moon,
Slide banisters of sunbeams,
You'll grow up far too soon.

Until then, sky baby,
We'll spread our wings and fly
And show you all the wonders
Of the never-ending skies.

Maureen Haselhurst

Nine amazing planets

Nine amazing planets.
Round and round they spin.
That's our solar system:
Where does it begin?

Mercury and Venus
Circle round the Sun,
Next the Earth comes twirling,
Living there is fun!

Planet number four is
Mars, the bright red ball,
Then it's giant Jupiter,
Biggest of them all.

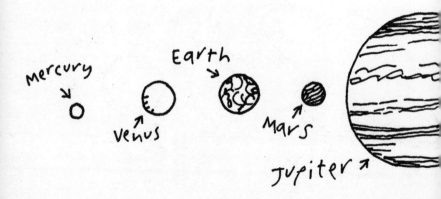

Saturn wears an ice belt,
Flat and thin and wide,
Further out, Uranus,
Tilting on its side.

Neptune is a beauty
With a big blue face,
And last is little Pluto,
A distant dot in space.

Darren Stanley

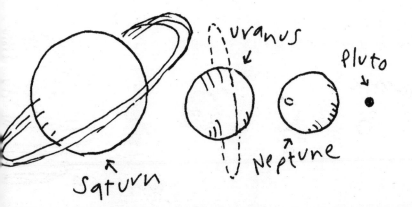

Constant, Constant Little Light

(A twenty-first-century version of Jane Taylor's poem "The Star", now universally known as the nursery rhyme "Twinkle, twinkle, little star")

Constant, constant little light,
catch my eye in darkest night.
What can speed so fast, so high,
laser-like across the sky?

When the sleepy sun has set
and the night has cast her net.
It's then your orbit forms a ring,
round the earth a song to sing.

Constant, constant little light,
I know you're a satellite.

Cruising, spinning, seldom seen,
beaming pictures to our screen.
Weather-watching, tracking storms,
plotting maps and all life forms.

Scanning, spying from above,
are you hawk or are you dove?
Silent, stealthy space-age Thor,
armed with weapons for a real star
    war.

From your tiny, silver glow,
who can tell what wrongs may flow?
But for now I hold you bright,
constant, constant little light.

Constant, constant little light,
I know you're a satellite.

John Rice

Janet's Planet Traffic Report

If you're heading for Saturn,
remember that it's down to
single lane on all the ring roads.
Resurfacing work continues on the
   Milky Way.
A meteor shower in the vicinity of
   Venus
is making flying conditions difficult.

A space transporter has jack-knifed
    on
The Neptune bypass and there are
    queues
back as far as Pluto.
And, as usual, look out for black holes
    in the road
on the very edge of the galaxy.
Finally, a reminder to all travellers
    entering
Earth's atmosphere.
Please drive on the left when passing
    England.

John Coldwell

Thank-you Letter

Dear Sun,

Just a line to say:
Thanks for this
And every day.
Your dawns and sunsets
Are just great –
Bang on time,
Never late.
On dismal days,
As grey as slate,
Behind a cloud
You calmly wait,
Till out you sail
With cheerful grace
To put a smile
On the whole world's face.
Thanks for those
Blazing days on beaches,
For ripening apples,
Pears and peaches;

For sharing out
Your noble glow;
For sunsets –
The loveliest things I know
Please carry on:
We know your worth.

Love from
A Friend on Planet Earth

Eric Finney

Garage Sale in Outer Space

They're having a big sale in outer
    space –
There are wonderful deals to be had,
Like a five-eyed pair of spectacles
For a pound, which isn't bad.

There are supersonic tennis balls,
Black holes in every size,
Plus squirming tendril cleansing
    soap –
Green rocks that harmonize,

A make-up kit for thorny skin,
A robot brain replacer,
Some deep-messaging bubble bath,
A hairy wart eraser.

A flesh-dissolving laser gun,
Some antimatter mints,
A bucket full of rocket fuel,
Some Martian red hair rinse,

A flying saucer license plate,
A mountain levitator,
Pet meteors and creeping goop,
A "Thing" disintegrator.

The sales are great – out of this world;
You'll want to go today.
But just be sure you pack a lunch –
It's a million miles away!

Robert Scotellaro

A saucer of creatures from Mars

A saucer of creatures from Mars
Set off on a night filled with stars,
They left at a streak
But were back in the week
For they missed their mamas and
    papas.

Philip Waddell

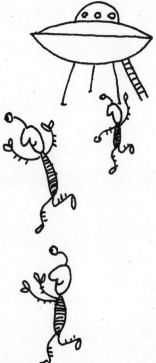